10-MINUTE BRAIN GAMES for Clever Kids

Puzzles and solutions
by Dr Gareth Moore
B.Sc (Hons) M.Phil Ph.D

Cover artwork by Chris Dickason
Illustrations by Nikalas Catlow

Designed by Zoe Bradley and Jack Clucas
Edited by Katy Lennon and Sophie Schrey
Cover Design by Angie Allison

First published in Great Britain in 2019 by Buster Books,
an imprint of Michael O'Mara Books Limited,
9 Lion Yard, Tremadoc Road, London SW4 7NQ

 www.mombooks.com/buster

 Buster Books

@BusterBooks

This book contains material previously published in
Kids' 10-Minute Brain Workout and *The Kids' Book of Puzzles 1*

A CIP catalogue record for this book is available from the British Library.

ISBN: 978-1-78055-593-5

4 6 8 10 9 7 5 3

Papers used by Buster Books are natural, recyclable products made of wood from
well-managed, FSC®-certified forests and other controlled sources. The manufacturing
processes conform to the environmental regulations of the country of origin.

Printed and bound in January 2020 by CPI Group (UK) Ltd,
108 Beddington Lane, Croydon, CR0 4YY, United Kingdom

10-MINUTE BRAIN GAMES for Clever Kids

Buster Books

INTRODUCTION

Are you ready for a brain workout? This book contains 90 ten-minute brain games, which are designed to test every part of your brain and maximize your mental powers. Did you know that your brain has up to double the learning power of an adult's brain? As you get older, parts of your brain that you don't use regularly begin to fade away — just the same as the muscles in your body become weaker if you don't exercise.

There is one complete brain game on every page. Try to do one or two pages a day and to finish each page in under ten minutes. There is space for you to write how much time it took you to complete each game at the top of the page.

10-Minute Brain Games for Clever Kids can help improve your memory, language skills, numeracy, concentration, and visual and spatial awareness. Upgrading your thinking will improve your performance at school and help you feel better throughout the day whatever you're doing — whether it's playing sports, solving a problem or even just chatting. The more you use your brain, the cleverer you will become!

This book is a brilliant start to improving your brain, but there are also other things that you can do to help. Your brain is a part of your body so for it to be in top condition it is vital that you look after your body too:

1) Take regular physical exercise. This will get your blood pumping oxygen to your brain and you'll think more clearly.

2) Sleep well. Most people need at least eight hours sleep per night. Some need less and some need more. But if you don't get enough for you then your brain won't be able to function to its full potential.

3) Eat breakfast. A bowl of cereal or piece of toast in the morning will help your body wake up and will provide the energy your brain needs to function during the day.

4) Drink plenty of water. It's difficult to think clearly when you're dehydrated, so make sure that you keep yourself topped up with water whenever you feel thirsty.

5) Eat a healthy, balanced diet. Foods that are especially good for your brain include fresh fruit and vegetables, nuts, eggs, lean meat and oily fish such as mackerel, salmon, trout and tuna (though avoid any of these foods if you are allergic to them).

As well as tackling the brain games in this book, you can invent your own mental challenges throughout the day. You could start from the moment you get up in the morning by eating your cereal with your other hand, and finish by learning a new word from a dictionary just before you go to sleep.

Tactical games such as chess, cards or dominoes can improve your concentration, reasoning and memory skills. Reading is very good for your brain as it helps you learn new words and phrases, improves your memory and helps you make sense of the world around you. There are all sorts of things you can do to increase your brain powers, and you can start right now with this book.

Every game can be solved by thinking carefully about the problem in front of you. You should never need to guess in order to complete the game. All you'll need to solve the puzzles in this book is a pencil – and your brain!

Don't be afraid to make notes or write on the pages – this can be a good tactic to help you keep track of your thoughts as you work on a puzzle. There are some blank pages at the back of the book that you can use for working out your answers.

Check your answers at the back of the book. If you're finding it difficult to complete an exercise, it is okay to take a quick peek at the answers. Even when you have seen the answer it can still be a challenge to work out how to get there.

Remember... you are training your brain so it's the thinking along the way that's important, not the answer itself.

To keep up with your increasing brain power, the brain games get steadily harder as you progress through the book. It's best to start at the beginning and work your way through, because sometimes the earlier puzzles will give you hints and tips that will help you with the later puzzles.

Are you ready to take the first step towards improving your brain power? Then turn to Brain Game 1, and enjoy!

Introducing the Brain Games Master:
Gareth Moore, B.Sc (Hons) M.Phil Ph.D

Dr Gareth Moore is an Ace Puzzler, and author of lots of puzzle and brain-training books.

He created an online brain-training site called BrainedUp.com, and runs an online puzzle site called PuzzleMix.com. Gareth has a Ph.D from the University of Cambridge, where he taught machines to understand spoken English.

Let the BRAIN GAMES begin!

Complete this sudoku puzzle by placing a number from 1 to 6 in every square, but with no number appearing more than once in each row, column or marked two-by-three area.

	3		6	2	
		5	2	6	
			1		
		1			
	4	2	5		
	2	6		3	

Find the fruits in the wordsearch square below. They might be written forwards, backwards, up, down or diagonally.

BANANA	LIME	PEAR
BLACKBERRY	MELON	PINEAPPLE
GRAPE	NECTARINE	RASPBERRY
KIWI	ORANGE	SATSUMA
LEMON	PEACH	STRAWBERRY

Y	P	M	L	Y	R	N	N	S	N
R	R	I	M	R	E	O	A	A	E
R	M	R	N	R	M	L	K	T	C
E	R	E	E	E	C	E	I	S	T
B	B	P	L	B	A	M	W	U	A
P	E	A	R	K	W	P	I	M	R
S	R	R	N	C	E	A	P	A	I
A	E	G	N	A	R	O	R	L	N
R	M	R	C	L	N	C	R	T	E
U	R	H	L	B	P	A	A	L	S

An anagram is a word that can be made by rearranging the letters of another word.

For example, DOG is an anagram of GOD.

Unscramble the anagrams below to fill in the missing words in these sentences. Each missing word is an anagram of the word written in capital letters in the same sentence.

a) Her favourite fruits are LEMONS and _____.

b) He _____ his car to DOVER.

c) He rode a HORSE along the _____.

d) When I eat LIMES, I get a _____ on my face.

e) Take CARE when driving a _____ car.

f) ROSE thorns can make your finger _____!

g) Every time you visit ROME, you find _____ to do.

h) My uncle is a BORE who wears a purple_____.

i) At EASTER we'll drive a five-_____ car.

j) '_____ keepers,' she said to her FRIENDS.

k) The men in the MANORS were held for _____.

l) Witches have OPTIONS when mixing _____.

m) She ate it then STATED that it _____ funny!

n) Wait in the _____ for the sauce to THICKEN.

Find the following battleships hidden within the grids:

1 x Cruiser

2 x Destroyers

2 x Submarines

THE RULES

- Each row and column has a number next to it indicating how many ship segments are in that row or column.
- Ships cannot be placed diagonally.
- Ships cannot touch directly to the left, right, top or bottom (though they can touch diagonally).

Puzzle A

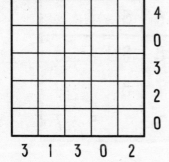

4
0
3
2
0

3 1 3 0 2

Puzzle B

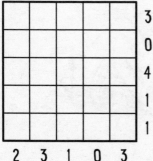

3
0
4
1
1

2 3 1 0 3

Complete this sudoku puzzle by placing a number from 1 to 9 in every square, but with no number appearing more than once in each row, column or marked three-by-three area.

8	1		5	2			3	6
6		2	7		1	4		
9	7	3	8	6			1	
	4	9	1		5		6	
5	6		3		2		8	4
	2		9		6	5	7	
	9			5	8	6	4	3
		5	6		7	8		9
2	8			9	3		5	7

Fit all these animal noises into the crossword. They can be written forwards or downwards.

BUZZ	GROWL	MEOW	RIBBIT
CHIRP	HISS	OINK	ROAR
CROAK	HOWL	PURR	SQUEAK
CUCKOO	HUM	QUACK	WOOF

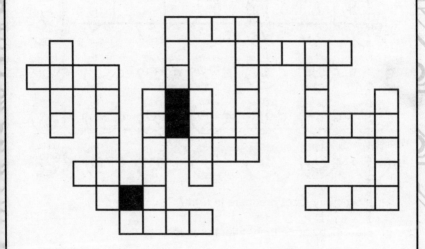

Five letters from the alphabet aren't used in this puzzle. What are they?

 TIME ....

Look at all these cartoon faces!

a) How many faces are there in total?

b) How many are either smiling or laughing?

c) How many have one eye closed and one eye open?

d) How many open eyes are there in total?

e) Without counting, work out how many closed eyes there must be.

f) How many are either wearing glasses or sticking out their tongue?

g) How many are both wearing glasses and sticking out their tongue?

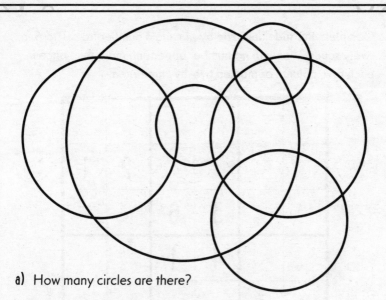

a) How many circles are there?

b) How many different sizes of circle are there?

c) How many points are there where the lines of the circles cross?

d) Where the circles overlap, new non-circular shapes are made (which do not overlap). If you wanted to colour each of these shapes a different colour, how many colours would you need?

e) What is the least number of colours you would need to colour the non-circular shapes so that no shapes of the same colour touch at any point including their corners?

Complete this sudoku puzzle by placing a number from 1 to 6 in every square, but with no number appearing more than once in each row, column or marked two-by-three area.

				2	1
		3	6		
		4	1		
2	3				

Decipher this back-to-front story about computers and answer the questions below.

a) In what year was the first computer invented?

b) How much did ENIAC weigh?

c) What was the original name of Charles Babbage's computer?

d) In which country was ENIAC built?

e) What non-electrical technology did Charles Babbage's machine use?

The first computer was invented by a British man called Charles Babbage in 1855. It didn't use electricity like modern machines, but instead had a large number of mechanical cogs. He called it a 'difference engine' because it could solve complex sums. Although Babbage never finished building it, it was the beginning of the birth of computing. It was designed to work out tables of mathematical results. At the time, people employed to work out these tables of results were called 'computers,' so the name became attached to Babbage's difference engine, and we still use the term today.

The first general-purpose and fully electronic computer was built in the United States. It was called ENIAC, and was finished in 1946. It was the size of a house and weighed 30 tons. It required as much power to run as an entire town.

Complete these slitherlink puzzles by 'slithering' a line around each grid to link up some of the dots.

THE RULES

- The line must form one complete loop and use only horizontal and vertical lines to join the dots.
- The loop cannot cross or touch itself in any way.
- Each 'square' with a number in it must have precisely that many of its sides completed with a line between the dots. So a '1' has a line between the dots on one of its sides, but no lines on its other three sides.
- If there is no number in a square, it may have as many or as few sides completed as you need.

Here's a solved puzzle to help you understand:

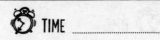

Puzzle A

Puzzle B

Puzzle C

Complete these hashi puzzles by correctly connecting the wires to the terminals on the circuits.

THE RULES

- Between any pair of terminals, there can be either ONE wire, TWO wires or NO connection.
- Each terminal is numbered, telling you how many wires in total connect to it.
- All wires must connect directly vertically or horizontally, but not diagonally or with a bend.
- No two wires can cross one another.
- Wires cannot go over or under a terminal. The completed circuit connects in such a way that an electric current can reach every terminal by running through the wires.

Here's a solved puzzle to help you understand:

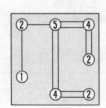

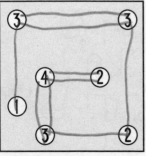

Puzzle A

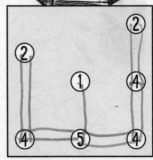

Puzzle B

The three pieces missing from this jigsaw are mixed up with some pieces from another jigsaw. Can you find the three pieces needed to go in the gaps?

There are 28 dominoes in a pack, each with two halves. Each half is either blank or has from one to six dots. No two dominoes are the same, and all possible combinations are found in a pack. Which three dominoes are missing from this pack?

The missing dominoes are:

Using just three straight lines, divide the goldfish bowl into six areas, each area containing one fish and one bubble.

Complete this sudoku puzzle by placing a number from 1 to 9 in every square, but with no number appearing more than once in each row, column or marked three-by-three area.

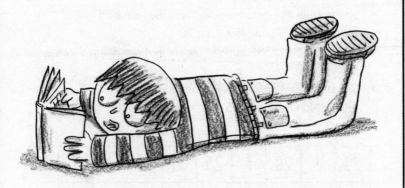

3	7	8		4		6	9	
6					8			7
	2	1	9				3	
8	5	6	4				2	
	3		2		1		4	
	4				7	9	8	3
	1				3	2	6	
9			6					4
	6	7		1		3	5	9

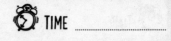
Shade the following squares in this grid:

- Shade squares containing even numbers. Even numbers are those in the 2-times table (2, 4, 6 and so on).
- Shade squares containing numbers that are both greater than 10 and less than 20.
- Shade squares containing numbers that are in the 3-times table (3, 6, 9 and so on).
- Shade squares containing numbers that are in the 5-times table. (Numbers in the 5 times table end in 0 or 5.)

29	1	29	7	23	31	29	1	7	18
23	53	31	43	1	53	43	23	85	13
37	41	1	37	43	49	31	20	19	65
7	29	7	23	29	1	50	5	70	95
23	2	31	49	53	23	22	27	55	23
90	24	8	53	1	84	16	17	43	49
12	15	3	18	40	15	6	47	41	37
1	30	21	15	14	4	22	37	29	7
29	7	13	14	62	9	23	31	53	23
43	23	37	25	12	7	49	29	31	1

Can you spot ten subtle differences between these two pictures?

Complete these kakuro puzzles:

THE RULES

- Place numbers from 1 to 9 in all the white squares.
- You must place the numbers so that each continuous run of white squares adds up to the total shown to the left or to the top of it (in the light-grey squares).
- You cannot repeat a number in any continuous run of white squares. For example, to make the total '4' you would have to use '1' and '3', since '2' and '2' would mean repeating '2'.

Puzzle A

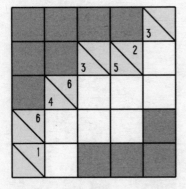

Puzzle B

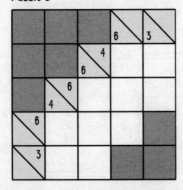

Find the action words in the wordsearch square below. They might be written forwards, backwards, up, down or diagonally.

BANG	KABOOM	SMASH	WHIZ
BIFF	KACHOW	SNIKT	ZANG
BLAM	KERSPLAT	THOK	ZAP
BOP	KROOM	THWUNK	ZOWIE
CRUNCH	OOF	WAP	
EEYOW	POW	WHAM	

Z	A	N	G	P	K	K	U	S	O	B
U	H	A	S	N	I	K	T	N	P	H
P	S	H	H	B	A	H	A	S	W	S
M	A	T	P	C	O	B	L	A	M	Y
O	M	Z	H	O	N	H	P	N	T	K
I	S	O	F	W	W	U	S	I	H	B
W	W	W	O	O	U	K	R	O	O	M
H	S	I	Y	B	M	N	E	C	K	O
A	H	E	I	O	A	Y	K	U	A	N
H	E	F	T	P	H	K	P	W	S	Y
E	F	O	I	E	W	H	I	Z	N	P

 TIME ....

Complete this sudoku puzzle by placing a number from 1 to 6 in every square, but with no number appearing more than once in each row, column or marked two-by-three area.

1					6
	3				4
			2	5	
	6	1			
2				1	
4					5

Each word ladder has a word at the top and another at the bottom. Join the bottom word to the top word by placing a new word above each step.

THE RULES

- Only one letter changes at each step, and it can change to any letter in the alphabet.
- Only words from the English dictionary can be used.

For example, join MAT to COT like this: MAT, CAT, COT.

Complete these slitherlink puzzles by 'slithering' a line around each grid to link up some of the dots.

THE RULES

- The line must form one complete loop and use only horizontal and vertical lines to join the dots.
- The loop cannot cross or touch itself in any way.
- Each 'square' with a number in it must have precisely that many of its sides completed with a line between the dots. So a '1' has a line between the dots on one of its sides, but no lines on its other three sides.
- If there is no number in a square, it may have as many or as few sides completed as you need.

Puzzle A

3	2	3
2	3	2
2	2	2

Here's a solved puzzle to help you understand:

1		3
3		1
1		3

Puzzle B

3	2	2	1
3	1		2
2		3	3
3	2	0	1

Puzzle C

3	2	0	0
2	2		1
3		3	3
3	1	2	2

Can you spot these two pirates in the crowd?

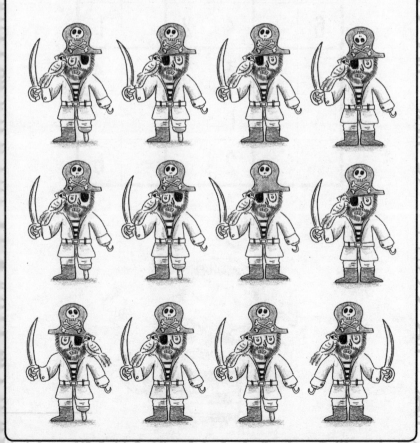

Complete this sudoku 'X' puzzle by placing a number from 1 to 6 in every square, but with no number appearing more than once in each row, column, marked two-by-three area, or on either of the two shaded diagonals.

3			1		
			3	6	
6		4	2		1
2		3	5		4
	4	1			
		2			6

Break the top-secret codes to reveal the hidden messages. Code Two is actually a hoax, designed to fool an enemy if the message is intercepted. The real message can be discovered by cracking Code Three, but you will need to crack Codes One and Two first.

CODE ONE
Each letter has been replaced by the letter that comes two before it in the alphabet. So C is written as A, D is written as B, and so on.

UCJJ BMLC ML BCAMBGLE RFGQ!

CODE TWO
Every other letter is false (the second, fourth, sixth, etc.).

SKEMCLRIECTW MGAQP YHZIMDSDRERNM INNM GSALRADCE!N

CODE THREE
Take the false letters from Code Two, then decipher the secret message by applying Code One.

 TIME ....

Find the following battleships hidden within the grids:

1 x Cruiser

2 x Destroyers

2 x Submarines

THE RULES

- Each row and column has a number next to it indicating how many ship segments are in that row or column.
- Ships cannot be placed diagonally.
- Ships cannot touch directly to the left, right, top or bottom (though they can touch diagonally).

Puzzle A

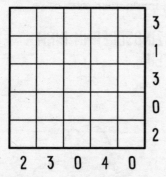

3
1
3
0
2

2 3 0 4 0

Puzzle B

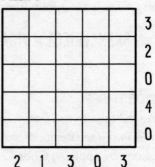

3
2
0
4
0

2 1 3 0 3

Puzzle C

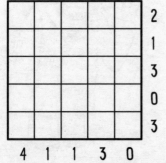

2
1
3
0
3

4 1 1 3 0

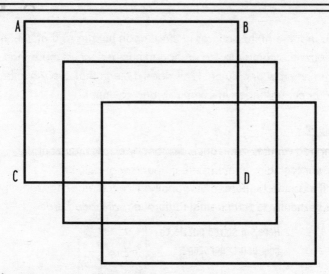

a) How many rectangles are there?
(Remember that squares are rectangles too.)

b) How many points are there where the lines
of the rectangles cross?

c) How many different sizes
of rectangle are there?

d) Where the large rectangles
overlap, new smaller shapes
are made (which do not overlap).
If you wanted to colour each
of these new shapes a different
colour, how many colours would
you need?

e) If you were to draw a line from
A to D and a line from B to C,
how many triangles of all
different sizes would there be?

Shade in some of the squares in these hitori puzzles so that, when each puzzle is complete, no unshaded number occurs more than once in any row or column. (This doesn't mean that every number has to occur unshaded in every row and column.)

THE RULES

- Shaded squares may touch diagonally but not horizontally or vertically.
- All unshaded squares must connect to each other horizontally or vertically to form a single unbroken, unshaded area.

Here's a solved puzzle to help you understand:

4	2	5	1	3
5	3	1	2	4
2	1	2	4	3
5	3	4	1	1
3	4	4	5	2

Puzzle A

2	1	3
3	3	3
3	2	1

Puzzle B

2	1	1
1	3	1
3	2	3

Complete this sudoku puzzle by placing a number from 1 to 6 in every square, but with no number appearing more than once in each row, column or marked two-by-three area.

			5	6	
		4		3	1
2	4		1		
	1	2			

These coins are from Moneyville, where people spend quiddles (q) and quoddles (Q). There are 100 quiddles (100q) in a quoddle (1Q). There are six types of coin:

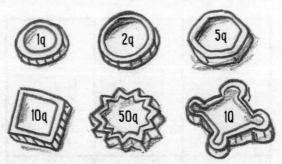

a) If you had one of each coin, how many quiddles would you have in total?

b) What is the least number of coins you would need to make up 1 quoddle without using the 1Q coin?

c) If you bought something costing 87q using a 1Q coin, what would be the least number of coins you could receive your change in?

d) You owe your friend 20 quiddles. What is the maximum number of coins you could pay him this money in if you were to give him no more than two of any coin size?

Using just three straight lines, divide the web into four areas, each area containing one spider and two flies.

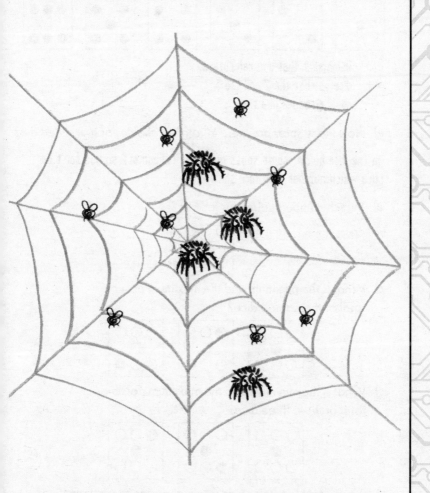

Clue: Only one line goes right the way across the web. The other two lines go from the edge of the web to one of the other lines.

Normal six-sided dice have spots on each face to represent a number from 1 to 6:

Remember that you can rotate dice so that the 2 and the 3 could also look like this:

a) How many spots are there in total on all sides of a six-sided die?

On the dice below, some spots may have rubbed off so you can't be sure which number each face shows:

b) Which numbers could this face be?

c) What is the minimum and the maximum possible total of these three dice?

d) What is the minimum and the maximum possible total of these three dice?

e) What possible totals could you make using these three dice?

Spot these two pots of flowers in the garden below.

Complete this sudoku 'X' puzzle by placing a number from 1 to 9 in every square, but with no number appearing more than once in each row, column, marked three-by-three area, or on either of the two shaded diagonals.

	2		7	4	6		3	9
	4	3	2					6
7	9		5	1		4	8	2
6			9	2	5		7	1
	1	7	8		4	6	2	
3	5		6	7	1			8
1	6	8		5	7		9	4
4					2	8	5	
2	3		4	8	9		6	

 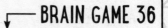

Complete each masyu puzzle by drawing a single loop that passes through the centre of every black or white circle.

- You can use only straight horizontal and vertical lines to draw the loop.
- The loop cannot enter any square more than once.
- At a BLACK circle, the loop must TURN then GO STRAIGHT on BOTH sides for at least one square.
- At a WHITE circle, the loop must GO STRAIGHT THROUGH then immediately TURN at ONE or BOTH of the squares on either side.
- In those squares that are not affected by a circle the loop can either go straight or turn.
- You do not have to use every empty square.

Puzzle A

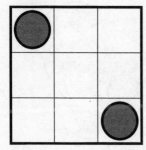

Here's a solved puzzle to help you understand:

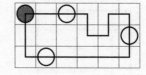

Puzzle B

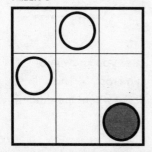

Shade squares in these hanjie puzzles to reveal the hidden images. The clues at the edge of each row and column reveal in order, from the left or from the top, the number of consecutive shaded squares in that row or column.

For example, a clue '2, 2' would mean there are two shaded squares touching, followed by a gap of at least one empty square, and then two more shaded squares touching.

Puzzle A

	1	1	5	3	1
1					
2					
5					
2					
1					

Puzzle A

Puzzle B

	1	3	5	3	1
1					
3					
5					
3					
1					

Puzzle B

Puzzle C

	2	2	1	2	2
	2	1	1	1	2
2, 2					
2, 2					
1					
1, 1					
5					

Puzzle C

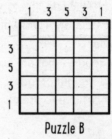

Puzzle D

	1	1		1	1
	1	2	3	2	1
1					
5					
1					
1, 1					
2, 2					

Puzzle D

Tip: Mark squares you know must be empty with a cross, 'x'. This will help you work out where the shaded squares go!

Find the vehicles in the wordsearch square below. They might be written forwards, backwards, up, down or diagonally.

AEROPLANE	MINIBUS	TANK
AMBULANCE	MOPED	TAXI
BICYCLE	MOTORBIKE	TRACTOR
BULLDOZER	ROCKET	TRAIN
CAR	SCOOTER	TRAM
COACH	SHIP	TRUCK
LORRY	STEAMROLLER	VAN

S	H	I	P	C	M	E	T	S	I	U
O	C	S	C	O	O	T	E	R	X	C
T	B	U	A	A	P	T	C	E	A	O
R	U	B	C	C	E	R	N	L	T	M
U	L	I	Y	H	D	A	A	C	R	C
C	L	N	R	C	L	I	L	Y	O	A
K	D	I	R	P	R	N	U	C	C	A
O	O	M	O	T	O	R	B	I	K	E
Z	Z	R	L	V	A	N	M	B	E	A
R	E	L	L	O	R	M	A	E	T	S
A	R	O	T	C	A	R	T	A	N	K

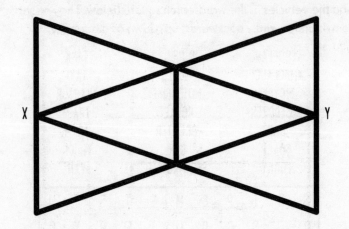

X   Y

a) How many triangles of all sizes are there?

b) How many different sizes of triangle are there?

c) What's the smallest total number of straight lines you could use to draw this diagram?

d) Is it possible to draw this diagram without taking your pen off the paper and without going over any line more than once?

e) If you drew a straight line from 'X' to 'Y', how many triangles of all sizes would there be?

Complete this irregular-area sudoku puzzle by placing a number from 1 to 6 in every square, but with no number appearing more than once in each row, column or marked six-square area.

2			4	5	6
3		5			2
4			2		3
6	2	4			5

Place eight dominoes where the double-blanks are to complete the domino chain.

THE RULES

- Dominoes can only touch one another when the number of pots on their touching ends match.
- You can only use the dominoes shown at the bottom of the page. You can only use each domino once.

Can you complete these kakuro puzzles?

THE RULES

- Place numbers from 1 to 9 in all the white squares.
- You must place the numbers so that each continuous run of white squares adds up to the total shown to the left or to the top of it (in the light-grey squares).
- You cannot repeat a number in any continuous run of white squares. For example, to make the total '4' you would have to use '1' and '3', since '2' and '2' would mean repeating '2'.

Puzzle A

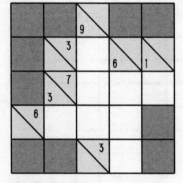

Puzzle B

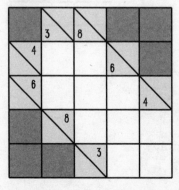

Fit all these vegetables into the crossword. They can be written forwards or downwards.

BEANS
BEETROOT
BROCCOLI
CABBAGE
CARROT
CELERY
CORN
COURGETTE

CRESS
LEEK
ONION
POTATO
SPROUT
SWEDE
TURNIP

Solve these nurikabe puzzles by shading in some of their squares.

THE RULES

- Each number must end up as part of a separate group of that number of unshaded squares.
- Groups of unshaded squares cannot touch horizontally or vertically (though they can touch diagonally).
- Shaded squares cannot form a two-by-two block.
- All the shaded squares must connect horizontally or vertically to form a single continuous area.

CORRECT

INCORRECT

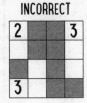

These shaded squares do not all connect vertically or horizontally and there is a shaded two-by-two block.

Puzzle A

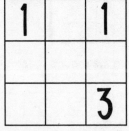

Puzzle B

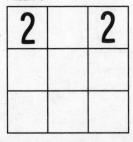

Complete this wordoku puzzle by placing one of the following letters in every square, but with no letter appearing more than once in each row, column or marked two-by-three area.

N R K B A I

		N			
A			R		
	B				K
	K			I	
		R			B
			N		

Find the hidden word by reading the letters in the shaded squares from left to right and top to bottom.

The four pieces missing from this jigsaw are mixed up with pieces from another jigsaw. Can you find the four pieces needed to go in the gaps?

Each word ladder has a word at the top and another at the bottom. Join the bottom word to the top word by placing a new word above each step.

THE RULES
- Only one letter changes at each step, and it can change to any letter in the alphabet.
- Only words from the English dictionary can be used.

For example, join MAT to COT like this: MAT, CAT, COT.

HEAD

BEAD

BAND

GOLD

COIN

ROAD

LARD

LANE

Complete these slitherlink puzzles by 'slithering' a line around each grid to link up some of the dots.

THE RULES

- The line must form one complete loop and use only horizontal and vertical lines to join the dots.
- The loop cannot cross or touch itself in any way.
- Each 'square' with a number in it must have precisely that many of its sides completed with a line between the dots. So a '1' has a line between the dots on one of its sides, but no lines on its other three sides.
- If there is no number in a square, it may have as many or as few sides completed as you need.

Puzzle A

```
1  0  0  0
3  2     0
1     2  1
2  1  2  3
```

Here's a solved puzzle to help you understand:

```
1        3
   3     1
   1     3
```

```
2  1  1  2
1        2
1        3
3  3  2  3
```

Puzzle B

Puzzle C

```
2  2  3  3
1     2     2
1  2     1  3
3     2     3
   1  3  1  3
```

Shade in some of the squares in these hitori puzzles so that, when each puzzle is complete, no unshaded number occurs more than once in any row or column. (This doesn't mean that every number has to occur unshaded in every row and column.)

THE RULES

- Shaded squares may touch diagonally but not horizontally or vertically.
- All unshaded squares must connect to each other horizontally or vertically to form a single unbroken, unshaded area.

Here's a solved puzzle to help you understand:

4	2	5	1	5
5	3	1	2	4
2	1	2	4	3
5	3	4	1	1
3	4	4	5	2

Puzzle A

3	1	2
2	3	1
2	1	1

Puzzle B

2	2	3
1	1	2
2	3	1

Puzzle C

1	1	3
3	3	2
2	3	1

Complete this sudoku 'X' puzzle by placing a number from 1 to 9 in every square, but with no number appearing more than once in each row, column, marked three-by-three area, or on either of the two shaded diagonals.

3		2	5	9		7		
9		8	7	2	3		4	5
	5					3		
			4		8			6
4	6		1		7		3	2
8			2		9			
		6					5	
5	9		3	8	2	1		7
		3		1	5	4		8

 TIME ....

Find the following battleships hidden within the grids:

1 x Cruiser

2 x Destroyers

2 x Submarines

THE RULES

- Each row and column has a number next to it indicating how many ship segments are in that row or column.
- Ships cannot be placed diagonally.
- Ships cannot touch directly to the left, right, top or bottom (though they can touch diagonally).

Puzzle A

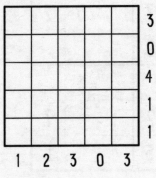

3
0
4
1
1

1 2 3 0 3

Puzzle B

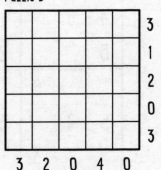

3
1
2
0
3

3 2 0 4 0

Puzzle C

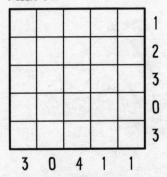

1
2
3
0
3

3 0 4 1 1

a) How many stick figures have at least one arm up in the air?

b) How many have both feet facing the same way?

c) How many are both smiling and holding their arms in a U-shape that points either up or down?

d) How many have both arms pointing down and one foot up in the air?

e) How many have either their hands on their hips or are not smiling?

Break the top-secret codes to reveal the hidden messages. It may help to look at things back to front.

CODE ONE
Each vowel (A, E, I, O, U) has been replaced with the one that comes next in the alphabet. A is written as E, E is written as I, U is written as A, and so on.

DED YIO HAUR UBIOT THA WIIDAN CUR?
ET 'WIID' NIT GI!

CODE TWO
EHT DLOG SI DEIRUB NI EHT DRAY

CODE THREE
This message has been encrypted using Code Two. Each letter has then been replaced with the one that comes before it in the alphabet.

MTQ QNE QTNX DEHK!

Complete this sudoku puzzle by placing a number from 1 to 9 in every square, but with no number appearing more than once in each row, column or marked three-by-three area.

2	4					8	9	1
	6	7			3			
		9			2		3	
			3	8		1	4	
			1		9			
	8	2	4	7				
	7		6			2		
			2			3	1	
9	2	4					6	7

These two pictures are almost identical, with the bottom one being a mirror image of the top. However there are also ten differences between them – can you spot these?

Complete these hashi puzzles by correctly connecting the wires to the terminals on the circuits.

THE RULES

- Between any pair of terminals, there can be either ONE wire, TWO wires or NO connection.
- Each terminal is numbered, telling you how many wires in total connect to it.
- All wires must connect directly vertically or horizontally, but not diagonally or with a bend.
- No two wires can cross one another.
- Wires cannot go over or under a terminal.
- The completed circuit connects in such a way that an electric current can reach every terminal by running through the wires.

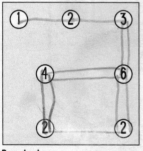

Here's a solved puzzle to help you understand:

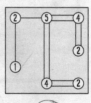

Puzzle A

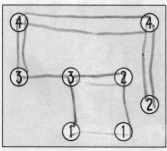

Puzzle B

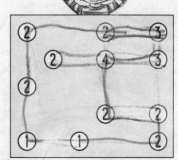

Puzzle C

Complete this irregular-area sudoku puzzle by placing a number from 1 to 6 in every square, but with no number appearing more than once in each row, column or marked six-square area.

	4	3	1		
5					1
2	3		6		
		2		3	6
1					3
		1	4	2	

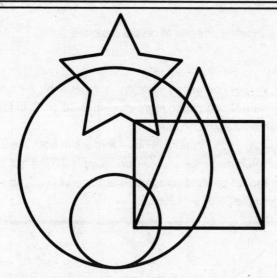

a) How many triangles are there?

b) Is it possible to draw this picture without taking your pen off the paper and without going along any line twice?

c) Where the big shapes overlap, new smaller shapes are made (which do not overlap). If you wanted to colour each of these new shapes a different colour, how many colours would you need?

d) What is the most sides that any polygon in this picture has? (A polygon is a shape made of straight lines that join up and don't cross over one another.)

Shade the shapes correctly to reveal a picture.

THE RULES

- Shade shapes containing numbers that are in the 7-times table.
- Shade shapes containing numbers with the digit '2' in them (for example 2, 12, 20 etc.).
- Shade shapes containing numbers that are in both the 2-times table AND the 5-times table (for example 10 but not 2 or 5).
- Shade shapes containing numbers that are in the 3-times table (for example 3, 6, 9, 12 etc.).

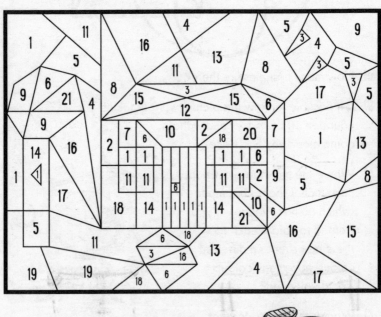

Complete these kakuro puzzles.

THE RULES

- Place numbers from 1 to 9 in all the white squares.
- You must place the numbers so that each continuous run of white squares adds up to the total shown to the left or to the top of it (in the light-grey squares).
- You cannot repeat a number in any continuous run of white squares. For example, to make the total '4' you would have to use '1' and '3', since '2' and '2' would mean repeating '2'.

Puzzle A

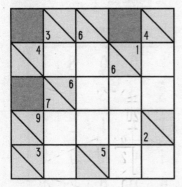

Puzzle B

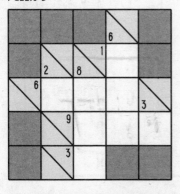

Find 'thank you' in many languages in the wordsearch square below. The words might be written forwards, backwards, up, down or diagonally.

ARIGATO (Japanese) KIITOS (Finnish)
DANKE (German) MERCI (French)
DEKUJI (Czech) OBRIGADO (Portuguese)
DOH JE (Cantonese) SPASIBO (Russian)
DZIEKUJE (Polish) TACK (Swedish)
EFHARISTO (Greek) TAKK (Norwegian)
GRACIAS (Spanish) TERIMA KASIH (Indonesian)
GRAZIE (Italian) TODA (Hebrew)

(You're not looking for the names of the languages.)

O	R	O	A	H	A	F	O	O	S	E
A	D	O	T	I	C	S	I	S	U	I
R	I	A	T	S	P	T	A	I	E	O
I	T	E	N	A	I	I	C	J	O	U
G	B	R	S	K	C	R	U	D	K	I
A	T	I	K	A	E	K	A	A	I	J
T	B	A	R	M	E	G	I	H	O	U
O	T	G	K	I	I	T	O	S	F	K
Z	G	D	Z	R	R	D	O	H	J	E
Z	A	D	B	E	I	Z	A	R	G	D
S	R	O	A	T	T	J	T	H	E	P

Complete this wordoku puzzle by placing one of the following letters in every square, but with no letter appearing more than once in each row, column or marked two-by-three area.

Z P L E S U

P					
					U
	E		S	L	Z
L	P	E		U	
S					
					P

Find the hidden word by reading the letters in the shaded squares from left to right and top to bottom.

These banknotes are from Moneyville, where people count their fortunes in quidillions (Qd). There are six types of banknote:

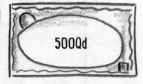

a) If you had one of each banknote, how many quidillions would you have?

b) If you bought something that cost 95Qd by giving the exact amount of money, what is the least number of banknotes that you could use to pay for it?

c) I have two of each banknote. How many banknotes will I have left if I buy something that costs 1365Qd?

d) If you only use the banknotes with numbers that start with '5', what is the least number of banknotes you can use to buy something that costs 1105Qd?

Complete each masyu puzzle by drawing a single loop that passes through the centre of every black or white circle.

THE RULES

- You can use only straight horizontal and vertical lines to draw the loop.
- The loop cannot enter any square more than once.
- At a BLACK circle, the loop must TURN then GO STRAIGHT on BOTH sides for at least one square.
- At a WHITE circle, the loop must GO STRAIGHT THROUGH then immediately TURN at ONE or BOTH of the squares on either side.
- In those squares that are not affected by a circle, the loop can either go straight or turn.
- You do not have to use every empty square.

Puzzle A

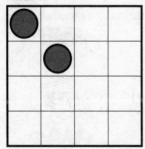

Here's a solved puzzle to help you understand:

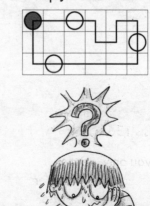

Puzzle B

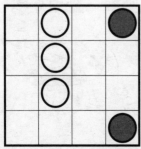

Spot these two monsters in the crowd.

Solve these nurikabe puzzles by shading in some of their squares.

THE RULES
- Each number must end up as part of a separate group of that number of unshaded squares.
- Groups of unshaded squares cannot touch horizontally or vertically (though they can touch diagonally).
- Shaded squares cannot form a two-by-two block.
- All the shaded squares must connect horizontally or vertically to form a single continuous area.

CORRECT

2		3	
3			

INCORRECT

2			3
3			

These shaded squares do not all connect vertically or horizontally and there is a shaded two-by-two block.

Puzzle A

2		
3		

Puzzle B

1			3
		1	
		2	

Complete this sudoku puzzle by placing a number from 1 to 9 in every square, but with no number appearing more than once in each row, column or marked three-by-three area.

1		5			6	3		
	3						6	
	9	6	3	7				5
	6	4	2	5				
	7						5	
				8	3	4	2	
3				4	7	2	9	
	4						8	
		1	8			6		7

An anagram is a word that can be made by rearranging the letters of another word.

For example, DOG is an anagram of GOD.

Unscramble the anagrams below to fill in the missing words in these sentences. Each missing word is an anagram of the word written in capital letters in the same sentence.

a) 'I like your coloured MARKERS,' _____ Sam.

b) He SECURED the boat and _____ the people.

c) Display NOTICES in this _____ of the shop.

d) You need good _____ to run on all TERRAINS.

e) NAMELESS _____ are forever telephoning me.

f) He TRIED hard to run, but he was too _____.

g) She SAVES her money to buy ceramic _____.

h) If you want to LISTEN it helps if you are _____.

i) The _____ caught the CHEATER.

j) On _____ we learnt about the DYNAMO.

k) Everyone AGREES that _____ is messy.

l) Which creepy-crawly is the NICEST _____?

m) He saw a scary THING in the dark that _____.

Using just four straight lines, divide the window into four areas, each area containing one rocket, one flying saucer and one star.

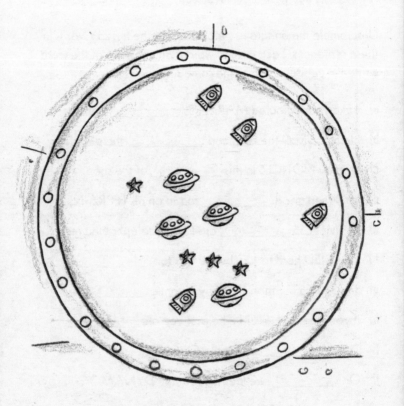

Clue: None of the lines go all the way from one side of the window to the other. They all run only from the edge of the circle to one of the other lines.

Complete this irregular-area sudoku puzzle by placing a number from 1 to 9 in every square, but with no number appearing more than once in each row, column or marked nine-square area.

9			1		3	4	6	
		6	5	4	9	2		8
	7				8			9
	1			6		3		2
6		4				1		7
3		1		2			5	
8			7				4	
2		3	4	8	1	7		
	4	7	6		5			3

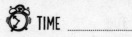

Complete this hashi puzzle by correctly connecting the wires to the terminals on the circuit:

THE RULES

- Between any pair of terminals, there can be either ONE wire, TWO wires or NO connection.
- Each terminal is numbered, telling you how many wires in total connect to it.
- All wires must connect directly vertically or horizontally, but not diagonally or with a bend.
- No two wires can cross one another.
- Wires cannot go over or under a terminal.
- The completed circuit connects in such a way that an electric current can reach every terminal by running through the wires.

Here's a solved puzzle to help you understand:

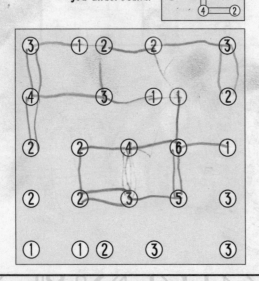

Break the top-secret codes to reveal the hidden messages.

CODE ONE
Each pair of letters has been swapped, so A B C D E F G H is
written B A D C F E H G.

ATEKISSXETSPAETSNAFDUOSRE
TSPONTRH

CODE TWO
Each letter has been replaced by a number representing its
position in the alphabet: A=1, B=2, and so on up to Z=26.

20 8 9 19 9 19 3 15 18 18 5 3 20
THISISCORRECT

CODE THREE
This message has been encrypted using Code Two from Brain
Game 26, then Code One from Brain Game 53. It has then
been flipped so that the whole message is back to front.

RNAOKTUTAHRIBSABDIITCORFATTHSEU
MMEUSASRAUGOEIOYK

Find the following battleships hidden within the grid:

1 x Aircraft carrier

1 x Battleship

1 x Cruiser

2 x Destroyers

3 x Submarines

THE RULES

- Each row and column has a number next to it indicating how many ship segments are in that row or column.
- Ships cannot be placed diagonally.
- Ships cannot touch directly to the left, right, top or bottom (though they can touch diagonally).

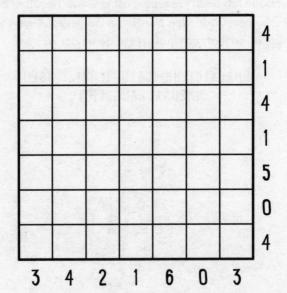

Complete this sudoku puzzle by placing a number from 1 to 9 in every square, but with no number appearing more than once in each row, column or marked three-by-three area.

4	1		7					
			4	1				9
8		7	9		2			3
		4				2	6	1
	9						7	
6	2	8				5		
7			2		9	1		5
1				6	5			
					1		2	6

These two pictures are almost identical, with the bottom one being an upside-down image of the top. However, there are ten differences between the two – can you spot them?

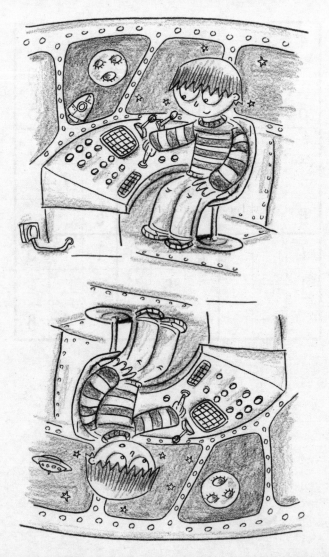

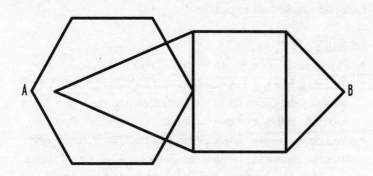

a) How many triangles are there?

b) How many quadrilaterals are there? (Quadrilaterals are shapes with four sides. The sides do not all have to be the same length.)

c) How many hexagons are there? (Hexagons are shapes with six sides. The sides do not all have to be the same length.)

d) Where the large shapes overlap, new smaller shapes are made (which do not overlap).If you wanted to colour each of these new shapes a different colour, how many colours would you need?

e) If you were to draw a line from A to B how many triangles would there then be?

Complete these kakuro puzzles.

THE RULES

- Place numbers from 1 to 9 in all the white squares.
- You must place the numbers so that each continuous run of white squares adds up to the total shown to the left or to the top of it (in the light-grey squares).
- You cannot repeat a number in any continuous run of white squares. For example, to make the total '4' you would have to use '1' and '3', since '2' and '2' would mean repeating '2'.

Puzzle A

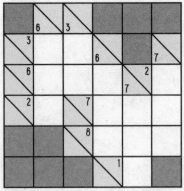

Puzzle B

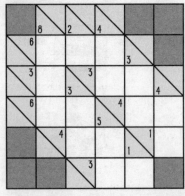

Decipher this muddled, back-to-front story about cinema and answer the questions below. Watch out, each pair of lines has been swapped, so that the second line comes before the first.

a) In what decade was photography introduced?

b) When were the first films with sound released?

c) What was the name of the first public system for playing back films?

d) What was the name of the brothers who demonstrated the first projector system? And when did they first reveal it?

photography in the 1830s,
Following the introduction of
playing a series of photographs
systems were developed for
the illusion that the picture was
in quick succession. This gave
in this way today. The first
moving, and cinema still works
reel of film with many pictures
public system to play back a
called the Kinetoscope, but it
on was revealed in 1893. It was
one person could watch the
was not very popular as only
the Lumière brothers
film at a time. In 1895, however,
Cinématographe projector
demonstrated their
cinema was born. Due to the
system in France, and modern
films were only a minute long.
lengths of film required, early
they were in black and white.
There was also no sound and
mainstream films in 1926, and in
Sound was first added to
produced. At this point colour
1934 the first colour films were
to make, and it was many
films were very expensive
widely available.
years before they were

Shade in some of the squares in these hitori puzzles so that, when each puzzle is complete, no unshaded number occurs more than once in any row or column.(This doesn't mean that every number has to occur unshaded in every row and column.)

THE RULES

- Shaded squares may touch diagonally but not horizontally or vertically.
- All unshaded squares must connect to each other horizontally or vertically to form a single unbroken, unshaded area.

Here's a solved puzzle to help you understand:

4	2	5	1	5
5	3	1	2	4
2	1	2	4	3
5	3	4	1	1
3	4	4	5	2

Puzzle A

2	3	3	4
1	1	2	3
3	2	3	1
4	1	4	2

Puzzle B

4	3	2	1
1	1	4	2
2	4	3	4
1	4	2	2

Complete this sudoku puzzle by placing a number from 1 to 9 in every square, but with no number appearing more than once in each row, column or marked three-by-three area.

		9	1			4	2	6
		3		8	5			
		4	2	6				
	2	6		5				
	3		4		8		2	
				2		7	5	
				1	9	3		
			6	4		8		
	5	2	8		3	1		

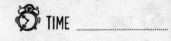
Complete these slitherlink puzzles by 'slithering' a line around each grid to link up some of the dots.

THE RULES

- The line must form one complete loop and use only horizontal and vertical lines to join the dots.
- The loop cannot cross or touch itself in any way.
- Each 'square' with a number in it must have precisely that many of its sides completed with a line between the dots. So a '1' has a line between the dots on one of its sides, but no lines on its other three sides.
- If there is no number in a square, it may have as many or as few sides completed as you need.

Here's a solved puzzle to help you understand:

```
1       3
   3    1
1       3
```

Puzzle A

```
2  1  1  3
1        3
1        2
2  2  3  3
```

Puzzle B

```
3  2  2  3  3  3
3  2     1  2  1
3  1  1  1     3
2     2  1  1  2
3  2  3        3  3
2  2  2  1  2  2
```

Find the cloud types below in the wordsearch square. They might be written forwards, backwards, up, down or diagonally.

ALTOCUMULUS   CIRRUS
ALTOSTRATUS   CUMULONIMBUS
CIRROCUMULUS   NIMBOSTRATUS
CIRROSTRATUS   STRATOCUMULUS

S	S	U	B	M	I	N	O	L	U	M	U	C	C
C	U	U	L	S	S	U	U	O	U	O	T	R
L	S	U	T	A	R	T	S	O	B	M	I	N	T
N	U	S	M	A	S	R	M	U	S	M	U	R	T
O	T	S	O	L	R	A	I	C	L	U	O	L	S
T	A	U	T	T	T	T	R	T	C	B	A	T	M
T	R	S	A	O	C	O	S	S	M	S	T	U	T
L	T	R	T	C	O	C	M	O	M	U	M	O	S
U	S	U	L	U	M	U	C	O	R	R	I	C	L
R	O	A	I	M	T	M	C	L	C	R	R	T	U
O	T	N	L	U	B	U	L	N	M	I	I	O	M
T	L	R	U	L	M	L	I	S	L	C	O	C	T
B	A	I	L	U	T	U	A	L	C	M	C	U	U
O	S	I	S	S	I	S	U	U	L	L	C	U	U

Shade squares in these hanjie puzzles to reveal the hidden images. The clues at the edge of each row and column reveal in order, from the left or from the top, the number of consecutive shaded squares in that row or column. For example, a clue '2, 2' would mean there are two shaded squares touching, followed by a gap of at least one empty square, and then two more shaded squares touching.

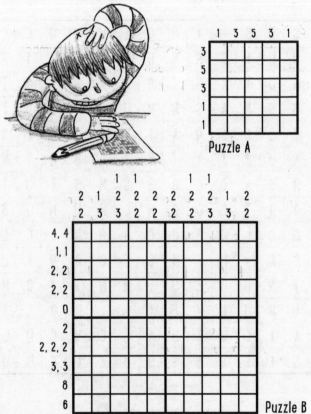

Puzzle A

Puzzle B

Tip: Mark squares you know must be empty with a cross, 'x'. This will help you work out where the shaded squares go.

Break the top-secret codes to reveal the hidden messages. When you've cracked Code Two, you will reveal a question that can be answered by cracking Code Three.

CODE ONE

Letters in this message have been coded to give numbers that represent their positions in the alphabet: A=1, B=2, and so on up to Z=26. However, these code numbers are not visible. Instead, the 'hidden' code numbers are the differences between the consecutive visible numbers. For example, the numbers '05 13' have a difference of 8 between them, and the eighth letter in the alphabet is 'H', so '05 13' is the code for 'H', and '05 13 04' is the code for 'HI'.

06 29 24 36 24 20 35 21 16

CODE TWO

This message has been coded so that every other letter, including the '?', is false (the first, third, fifth, etc.). These false letters, when read backwards, complete the message.

?WEHZYIDRIPDLTEHBEOCNOEWHWTIN

CODE THREE

Each consecutive pair of letters, including the '!', has been swapped around. For example A B C D is written B A D C.

EBACSUI EW TSA UOSTATDNNII
GI NST IFLE!D

Complete this irregular-area sudoku puzzle by placing a number from 1 to 9 in every square, but with no number appearing more than once in each row, column or marked nine-square area.

5	3	2	9					1
	6	4	7		9	3	5	
					8		6	3
4						2		
6	4	9	1		2	5	3	7
		1						5
2	9		8					
	2	8	3		6		1	7
1					3	8	2	9

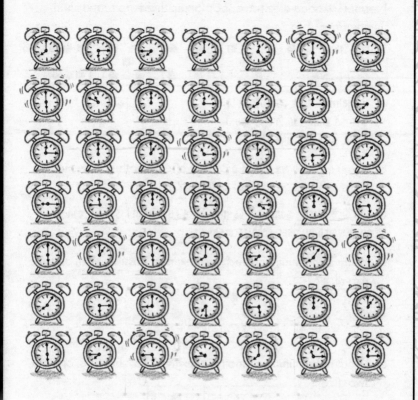

a) How many clocks are there?

b) How many are ringing?

c) How many show 15 minutes past the hour?

d) How many show 'quarter to' or 'o'clock'?

e) How many are showing either 11:15 or 8:05?

f) How many different times are there in total?

Normal six-sided dice have spots on each side to represent a number from 1 to 6:

Remember that you can rotate dice so that the 2 and the 3 ⟶ could also look like this:

a) If you roll two six-sided dice one after the other, how many ways can you get a total of seven?

On the dice below, some spots may have rubbed off so you can't be sure which number each face shows:

b) What is the minimum and the maximum possible total of these two dice?

c) What is the minimum and the maximum possible total of these two dice?

d) What different totals can you make with these two dice?

e) Using the same two dice as in (d), how many different doubles can you make? (A double is when you have two dice of the same value.)

Each word ladder has a word at the top and another at the bottom. Join the bottom word to the top word by placing a new word above each step.

THE RULES
- Only one letter changes at each step, and it can change to any letter in the alphabet.
- Only words from the English dictionary can be used.

For example, join MAT to COT like this: MAT, CAT, COT.

CAT

DOG

HIDE

FIND

LOOK

pigeon

moo

oink

SEES

This ladder contains clues to some of its steps.

Using just four straight lines, divide the field into five areas, each area containing one tree, one bush and one sheep.

Clue: Only one of the lines goes all the way from one side of the field to the other. The other three lines run only from the edge of the field to one of the other lines.

Complete this sudoku puzzle by placing a number from 1 to 9 in every square, but with no number appearing more than once in each row, column or marked three-by-three area.

3	9				6		4	1
				5				
7			1				5	2
2	6		8	7				
9				4				6
				9	1		3	4
4	7				8			9
				2				
8	1		7				2	3

All of the
ANSWERS

BRAIN GAME 1

5	3	4	6	2	1
4	1	5	2	6	3
2	6	3	1	5	4
6	5	1	3	4	2
3	4	2	5	1	6
1	2	6	4	3	5

BRAIN GAME 2

Y	P	M	L	Y	R	N	N	S	N
R	R	I	M	R	E	O	A	A	E
R	M	R	N	R	M	L	K	T	C
E	R	E	E	E	C	E	I	S	T
B	B	P	L	B	A	M	W	U	A
P	E	A	R	K	W	P	I	M	R
S	R	R	N	C	E	A	P	A	I
A	E	G	N	A	R	O	R	L	N
R	M	R	C	L	N	C	R	T	E
U	R	H	L	B	P	A	A	L	S

BRAIN GAME 3

a) Her favourite fruits are **LEMONS** and **MELONS**.

b) He **DROVE** his car to **DOVER**.

c) He rode a **HORSE** along the **SHORE**.

d) When I eat **LIMES**, I get a **SMILE** on my face.

e) Take **CARE** when driving a **RACE** car.

f) **ROSE** thorns can make your finger **SORE**!

g) Every time you visit **ROME**, you find **MORE** to do.

h) My uncle is a **BORE** who wears a purple **ROBE**.

i) At **EASTER** we'll drive a five-**SEATER** car.

j) '**FINDERS** keepers,' she said to her **FRIENDS**.

k) The men in the **MANORS** were held for **RANSOM**.

l) Witches have **OPTIONS** when mixing **POTIONS**.

m) She ate it then **STATED** that it **TASTED** funny!

n) Wait in the **KITCHEN** for the sauce to **THICKEN**.

BRAIN GAME 4

Puzzle A

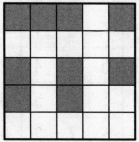

Puzzle B

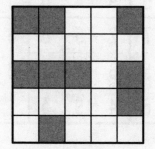

BRAIN GAME 5

8	1	4	5	2	9	7	3	6
6	5	2	7	3	1	4	9	8
9	7	3	8	6	4	2	1	5
7	4	9	1	8	5	3	6	2
5	6	1	3	7	2	9	8	4
3	2	8	9	4	6	5	7	1
1	9	7	2	5	8	6	4	3
4	3	5	6	1	7	8	2	9
2	8	6	4	9	3	1	5	7

BRAIN GAME 6

The five letters from the alphabet that aren't used
in this puzzle are **D**, **J**, **V**, **X** and **Y**.

BRAIN GAME 7

a) 49 faces
b) 27 faces
c) 12 faces
d) 66 eyes

e) 32 eyes (49 faces each with 2 eyes, minus 66 eyes)
f) 11 faces
g) 0 faces

BRAIN GAME 8

a) 6 circles
b) 4 different sizes
c) 16 points
d) 17 colours
e) 4 colours

BRAIN GAME 9

5	4	1	2	6	3
3	6	5	4	2	1
1	2	3	6	4	5
6	5	4	1	3	2
2	3	6	5	1	4
4	1	2	3	5	6

BRAIN GAME 10

a) The first computer was invented in **1822**.

b) ENIAC weighed **30 tons**.

c) Charles Babbage originally called his computer a **'difference engine'**.

d) ENIAC was built in the **United States**.

e) Babbage's machine used **mechanical cogs**.

BRAIN GAME 11

Puzzle A

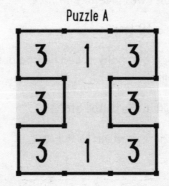

Puzzle B

Puzzle C

BRAIN GAME 12

Puzzle A

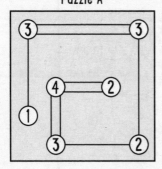

Puzzle B

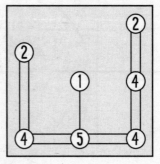

BRAIN GAME 13

BRAIN GAME 14

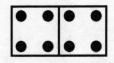

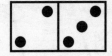

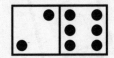

BRAIN GAME 15

BRAIN GAME 16

3	7	8	1	4	5	6	9	2
6	9	5	3	2	8	4	1	7
4	2	1	9	7	6	8	3	5
8	5	6	4	3	9	7	2	1
7	3	9	2	8	1	5	4	6
1	4	2	5	6	7	9	8	3
5	1	4	7	9	3	2	6	8
9	8	3	6	5	2	1	7	4
2	6	7	8	1	4	3	5	9

BRAIN GAME 17

29	1	29	7	23	31	29	1	7	18
23	53	31	43	1	53	43	23	85	13
37	41	1	37	43	49	31	20	19	65
7	29	7	23	29	1	50	5	70	95
23	2	31	49	53	23	22	27	55	23
90	24	8	53	1	84	16	17	43	49
12	15	3	18	40	15	6	47	41	37
1	30	21	15	14	4	22	37	29	7
29	7	13	14	62	9	23	31	53	23
43	23	37	25	12	7	49	29	31	1

BRAIN GAME 18

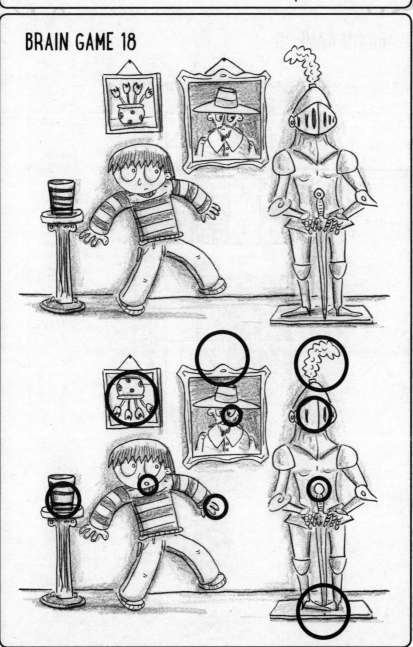

BRAIN GAME 19

Puzzle A

				3
		3	2 / 5	2
	4 / 6	2	3	1
6	3	1	2	
1	1			

Puzzle B

			6	3
		4 / 6	3	1
	4 / 6	3	1	2
6	3	1	2	
3	1	2		

BRAIN GAME 20

Z	A	N	G	P	K	K	U	S	O	B
U	H	A	S	N	I	K	T	N	P	H
P	S	H	H	B	A	H	A	S	W	S
M	A	T	P	C	O	B	L	A	M	Y
O	M	Z	H	O	N	H	P	N	T	K
I	S	O	F	W	W	U	S	I	H	B
W	W	O	O	U	K	R	O	O	M	M
H	S	I	Y	B	M	N	E	C	K	O
A	H	E	I	O	A	Y	K	U	A	N
H	E	F	T	P	H	K	P	W	S	Y
E	F	O	I	E	W	H	I	Z	N	P

BRAIN GAME 21

1	2	5	4	3	6
5	3	6	1	2	4
6	4	3	2	5	1
3	6	1	5	4	2
2	5	4	6	1	3
4	1	2	3	6	5

BRAIN GAME 22

MOO
BOO
BOA
BAA

BOY
BAY
BAN
MAN

BUS
BUT
CUT
CAT
CAR

Can you find any alternative solutions?

BRAIN GAME 23

Puzzle A

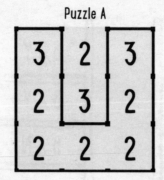

Puzzle B

Puzzle C

BRAIN GAME 24

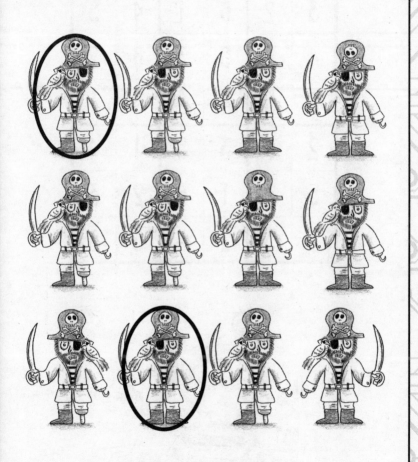

BRAIN GAME 25

3	2	6	1	4	5
4	1	5	3	6	2
6	5	4	2	3	1
2	6	3	5	1	4
5	4	1	6	2	3
1	3	2	4	5	6

BRAIN GAME 26

CODE ONE
WELL DONE ON DECODING THIS!

CODE TWO
SECRET MAP HIDDEN IN GARDEN

CODE THREE
MONKEY IS ABOUT TO POUNCE!

BRAIN GAME 27

Puzzle A

Puzzle B

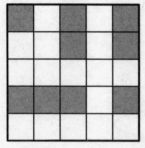

Puzzle C

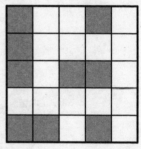

BRAIN GAME 28

a) **8** rectangles
b) **6** points
c) **4** different sizes
d) **7** colours
e) **15** triangles

BRAIN GAME 29

Puzzle A

2	1	3
3	3	3
3	2	1

Puzzle B

2	1	1
1	3	1
3	2	3

BRAIN GAME 30

4	3	1	6	2	5
1	2	3	5	6	4
6	5	4	2	3	1
2	4	6	1	5	3
5	1	2	3	4	6
3	6	5	4	1	2

BRAIN GAME 31

a) **168** quiddles
   (100q + 50q + 10q + 5q + 2q + 1q)
b) 2 coins (50q + 50q)
c) 3 coins (10q + 2q + 1q)
d) 5 coins (10q + 5q + 2q + 2q + 1q)

BRAIN GAME 32

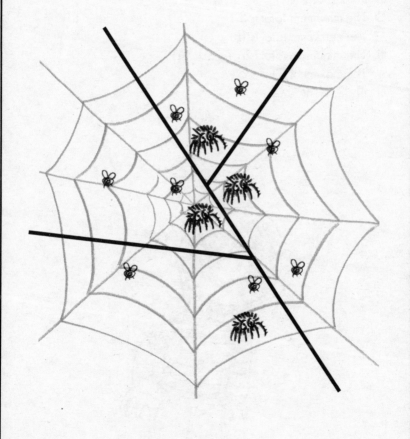

BRAIN GAME 33

a) 21 spots
b) 2, 3, 4, 5, 6
c) The minumum total is 5
   The maximum total is 17
d) The minumum total is 7
   The maximum total is 15
e) 10, 12, 14, 16

BRAIN GAME 34

BRAIN GAME 35

8	2	1	7	4	6	5	3	9
5	4	3	2	9	8	7	1	6
7	9	6	5	1	3	4	8	2
6	8	4	9	2	5	3	7	1
9	1	7	8	3	4	6	2	5
3	5	2	6	7	1	9	4	8
1	6	8	3	5	7	2	9	4
4	7	9	1	6	2	8	5	3
2	3	5	4	8	9	1	6	7

BRAIN GAME 36

Puzzle A

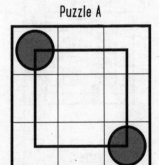

Puzzle B

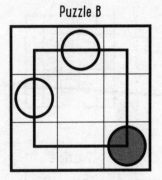

BRAIN GAME 37

Puzzle A

Puzzle B

Puzzle C

Puzzle D

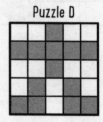

BRAIN GAME 38

S	H	I	P	C	M	E	T	S	I	U
O	C	S	C	O	O	T	E	R	X	C
T	B	U	A	A	P	T	C	E	A	O
R	U	B	C	C	E	R	N	L	T	M
U	L	I	Y	H	D	A	A	C	R	C
C	L	N	R	C	L	I	L	Y	O	A
K	D	I	R	P	R	N	U	C	C	A
O	O	M	O	T	O	R	B	I	K	E
Z	Z	R	L	V	A	N	M	B	E	A
R	E	L	L	O	R	M	A	E	T	S
A	R	O	T	C	A	R	T	A	N	K

BRAIN GAME 39

a) 8 triangles
b) 2 sizes
c) 7 straight lines
d) Yes
e) 18 triangles

BRAIN GAME 40

2	1	3	4	5	6
3	6	5	1	4	2
5	4	2	6	3	1
1	3	6	5	2	4
4	5	1	2	6	3
6	2	4	3	1	5

BRAIN GAME 41

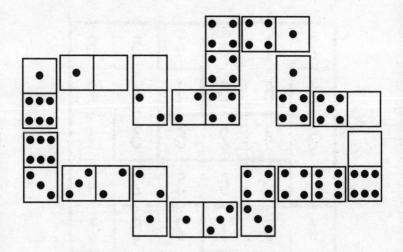

BRAIN GAME 42

Puzzle A

		9		
	3	3	6	1
	7	4	2	1
3				
6	3	2	1	
		3	3	

Puzzle B

	3	8		
4	1	3	6	
6	2	1	3	4
	8	4	1	3
		3	2	1

BRAIN GAME 43

```
    B E A N S         C           O
  B         P O T A T O     C     N
  R     C   R           C   O     I
  O     O   O           B E E T R O O T
  C     U   U           A       N   N
  C A R R O T           G     C
  O   G                 C E L E R Y
  L E E K                     E
  I   T                       S
    T U R N I P               S W E D E
      T
      E
```

BRAIN GAME 44

Puzzle A

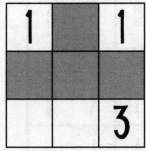

Puzzle B

BRAIN GAME 45

K	I	N	B	R	A
A	N	K	R	B	I
R	B	A	I	K	N
N	K	B	A	I	R
I	A	R	K	N	B
B	R	I	N	A	K

The hidden word is **BRAIN**.

BRAIN GAME 46

BRAIN GAME 47

HEAD
BEAD
BEND
BAND

GOLD
COLD
CORD
CORN
COIN

ROAD
LOAD
LORD
LARD
LAND
LANE

Can you find any alternative solutions?

BRAIN GAME 48

Puzzle A

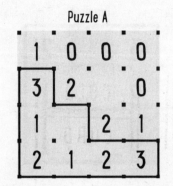

Puzzle B

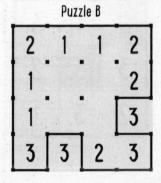

Puzzle C

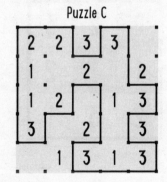

BRAIN GAME 49

Puzzle A

3	1	2
2	3	1
2	1	1

Puzzle B

2	2	3
1	1	2
2	3	1

Puzzle C

1	1	3
3	3	2
2	3	1

BRAIN GAME 50

3	4	2	5	9	6	7	8	1
9	1	8	7	2	3	6	4	5
6	5	7	8	4	1	3	2	9
2	7	5	4	3	8	9	1	6
4	6	9	1	5	7	8	3	2
8	3	1	2	6	9	5	7	4
1	8	6	9	7	4	2	5	3
5	9	4	3	8	2	1	6	7
7	2	3	6	1	5	4	9	8

BRAIN GAME 51

Puzzle A

Puzzle B

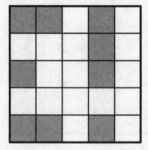

Puzzle C

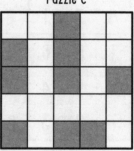

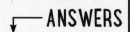

BRAIN GAME 52

a) 12 stick figures
b) 18 stick figures
c) 6 stick figures
d) 4 stick figures
e) 16 stick figures

BRAIN GAME 53

CODE ONE
DID YOU HEAR ABOUT THE WOODEN CAR?
IT 'WOOD' NOT GO!

CODE TWO
THE GOLD IS BURIED IN THE YARD

CODE THREE
RUN FOR YOUR LIFE!

BRAIN GAME 54

2	4	3	7	6	5	8	9	1
8	6	7	9	1	3	4	2	5
5	1	9	8	4	2	7	3	6
7	9	6	5	3	8	1	4	2
4	3	5	1	2	9	6	7	8
1	8	2	4	7	6	9	5	3
3	7	1	6	5	4	2	8	9
6	5	8	2	9	7	3	1	4
9	2	4	3	8	1	5	6	7

BRAIN GAME 55

BRAIN GAME 56

Puzzle A

Puzzle B

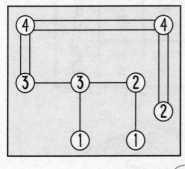

Puzzle C

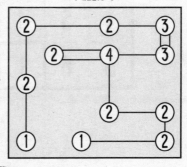

BRAIN GAME 57

6	4	3	1	5	2
5	2	6	3	4	1
2	3	5	6	1	4
4	1	2	5	3	6
1	5	4	2	6	3
3	6	1	4	2	5

BRAIN GAME 58

a) 5 triangles
b) Yes
c) 15 colours
d) 17 sides

BRAIN GAME 59

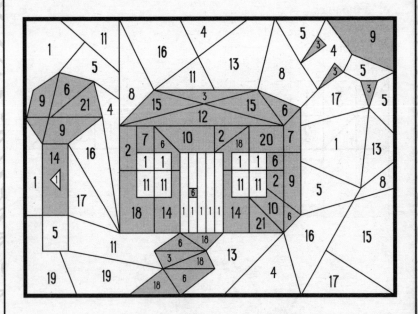

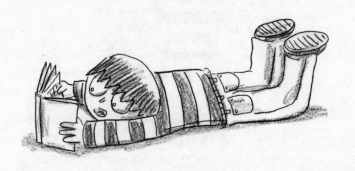

BRAIN GAME 60

Puzzle A

	3	6		4
4	3	1	1 / 6	1
7 / 6		2	1	3
9	4	3	2	/ 2
3	3	5	3	2

Puzzle B

			6	
	2	8	1	1
6	2	1	3	/ 3
	9	4	2	3
	3	3		

BRAIN GAME 61

O	R	O	A	H	A	F	O	O	S	E
A	D	O	T	I	C	S	I	S	U	I
R	I	A	T	S	P	T	A	I	E	O
I	T	E	N	A	I	I	C	J	O	U
G	B	R	S	K	C	R	U	D	K	I
A	T	I	K	A	E	K	A	A	I	J
T	B	A	R	M	E	G	I	H	O	U
O	T	G	K	I	I	T	O	S	F	K
Z	G	D	Z	R	R	D	O	H	J	E
Z	A	D	B	E	I	Z	A	R	G	D
S	R	O	A	T	T	J	T	H	E	P

BRAIN GAME 62

P	L	Z	U	S	E
Z	S	L	E	P	U
U	E	P	S	L	Z
L	P	E	Z	U	S
S	Z	U	P	E	L
E	U	S	L	Z	P

The hidden word is **PUZZLES**.

BRAIN GAME 63

a) 685Qd

b) 4 banknotes
   (50Qd + 20Qd + 20Qd + 5Qd)

c) 1 banknote (5Qd)

d) 5 banknotes
   (500Qd + 500Qd + 50Qd + 50Qd + 5Qd)

BRAIN GAME 64

Puzzle A

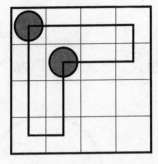

Puzzle B

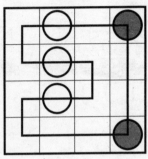

BRAIN GAME 65

BRAIN GAME 66

Puzzle A

2		
3		

Puzzle B

1			3
	1		
	2		

BRAIN GAME 67

1	8	5	4	9	6	3	7	2
7	3	2	5	1	8	9	6	4
4	9	6	3	7	2	8	1	5
8	6	4	2	5	1	7	3	9
2	7	3	9	6	4	1	5	8
5	1	9	7	8	3	4	2	6
3	5	8	6	4	7	2	9	1
6	4	7	1	2	9	5	8	3
9	2	1	8	3	5	6	4	7

BRAIN GAME 68

a) 'I like your coloured **MARKERS**,' **REMARKS** Sam.

b) He **SECURED** the boat and **RESCUED** the people.

c) Display **NOTICES** in this **SECTION** of the shop.

d) You need good **TRAINERS** to run on all **TERRAINS**.

e) **NAMELESS SALESMEN** are forever telephoning me.

f) He **TRIED** hard to run, but he was too **TIRED**.

g) She **SAVES** her money to buy ceramic **VASES**.

h) If you want to **LISTEN** it helps if you are **SILENT**.

i) The **TEACHER** caught the **CHEATER**.

j) On **MONDAY** we learnt about the **DYNAMO**.

k) Everyone **AGREES** that **GREASE** is messy.

l) Which creepy-crawly is the **NICEST INSECT**?

m) He saw a scary **THING** in the dark that **NIGHT**.

BRAIN GAME 69

BRAIN GAME 70

9	8	2	1	7	3	4	6	5
7	3	6	5	4	9	2	1	8
4	7	5	2	1	8	6	3	9
5	1	8	9	6	4	3	7	2
6	9	4	3	5	2	1	8	7
3	6	1	8	2	7	9	5	4
8	2	9	7	3	6	5	4	1
2	5	3	4	8	1	7	9	6
1	4	7	6	9	5	8	2	3

BRAIN GAME 71

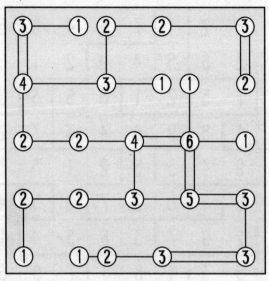

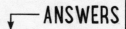

BRAIN GAME 72

CODE ONE
TAKE SIX STEPS EAST AND FOUR STEPS NORTH

CODE TWO
THIS IS CORRECT

CODE THREE
YOU ARE A MASTER CODE BREAKER

BRAIN GAME 73

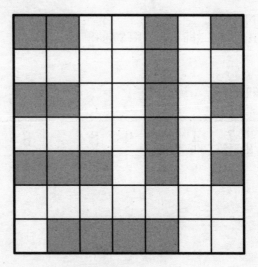

BRAIN GAME 74

4	1	9	7	8	3	6	5	2
2	5	3	4	1	6	7	8	9
8	6	7	9	5	2	4	1	3
3	7	4	5	9	8	2	6	1
5	9	1	6	2	4	3	7	8
6	2	8	1	3	7	5	9	4
7	8	6	2	4	9	1	3	5
1	3	2	8	6	5	9	4	7
9	4	5	3	7	1	8	2	6

BRAIN GAME 75

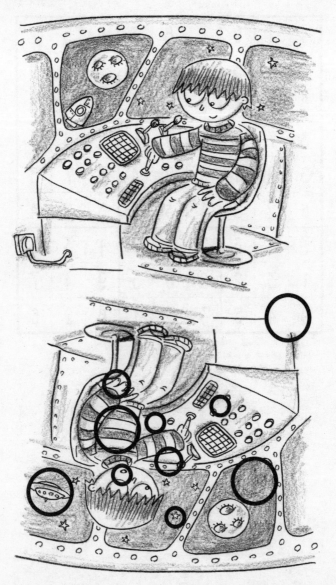

BRAIN GAME 76

a) 4 triangles
b) 4 quadrilaterals
c) 4 hexagons
d) 6 colours
e) 10 triangles

BRAIN GAME 77

Puzzle A

	6	3			
3	1	2	6		7
6	3	1	2	2	2
2	2	7	1	2	4
		8	3	4	1
			1	1	

Puzzle B

	8	2	4		
6	1	2	3	3	
3	3	3	1	2	4
6	4	2	4	1	3
	4	1	5	1	1
		3	2	1	

BRAIN GAME 78

a) Photography was introduced in the **1830s**.
b) The first films with sound were released in **1926**.
c) The name of the first public system for playing back films was the **Kinetoscope**.
d) **The Lumiére brothers** demonstrated the first projector system in 1895.

BRAIN GAME 79

Puzzle A

2	3	3	4
1	1	2	3
3	2	3	1
4	1	4	2

Puzzle B

4	3	2	1
1	1	4	2
2	4	3	4
1	4	2	2

BRAIN GAME 80

5	7	9	1	3	4	2	6	8
2	6	3	9	8	5	4	1	7
1	8	4	2	6	7	5	3	9
4	2	6	7	5	1	9	8	3
7	3	5	4	9	8	6	2	1
8	9	1	3	2	6	7	5	4
6	4	8	5	1	9	3	7	2
3	1	7	6	4	2	8	9	5
9	5	2	8	7	3	1	4	6

BRAIN GAME 81

Puzzle A

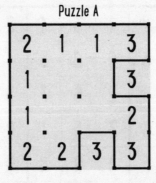

Puzzle B

BRAIN GAME 82

S	S	U	B	M	I	N	O	L	U	M	U	C	C
C	U	U	L	S	S	S	U	U	O	U	O	T	R
L	S	U	T	A	R	T	S	O	B	M	I	N	T
N	U	S	M	A	S	R	M	U	S	M	U	R	T
O	T	S	O	L	R	A	I	C	L	U	O	L	S
T	A	U	T	T	T	T	R	T	C	B	A	T	M
T	R	S	A	O	C	O	S	S	M	S	T	U	T
L	T	R	T	C	O	C	M	O	M	U	M	O	S
U	S	U	L	U	M	U	C	O	R	R	I	C	L
R	O	A	I	M	T	M	C	L	C	R	R	T	U
O	T	N	L	U	B	U	L	N	M	I	I	O	M
T	L	R	U	L	M	L	I	S	L	C	O	C	T
B	A	I	L	U	T	U	A	L	C	M	C	U	U
O	S	I	S	I	S	U	U	L	L	C	U	U	

BRAIN GAME 83

Puzzle A

Puzzle B

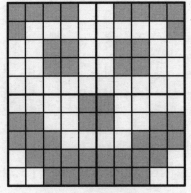

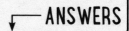

BRAIN GAME 84

CODE ONE
WELL DONE

CODE TWO
WHY DID THE COW WIN THE NOBEL PRIZE?

CODE THREE
BECAUSE IT WAS OUTSTANDING IN ITS FIELD!

BRAIN GAME 85

5	3	2	9	6	4	7	8	1
8	6	4	7	1	9	3	5	2
7	1	5	4	2	8	9	6	3
4	5	7	6	3	1	2	9	8
6	4	9	1	8	2	5	3	7
3	8	1	2	9	7	6	4	5
2	9	3	8	7	5	4	1	6
9	2	8	3	5	6	1	7	4
1	7	6	5	4	3	8	2	9

BRAIN GAME 86

a) 49 clocks
b) 6 clocks
c) 13 clocks
d) 29 clocks
e) 6 clocks
f) 18 different times

BRAIN GAME 87

a) 6 ways (1/6, 2/5, 3/4, 6/1, 5/2, 4/3)
b) The minimum total is 3
   The maximum total is 11
c) The minimum total is 7
   The maximum total is 11
d) 2, 4, 6, 8, 10
d) 3 doubles (1/1, 3/3, 5/5)

BRAIN GAME 88

CAT
COT
COG
DOG

HIDE
HIVE
FIVE
FINE
FIND

LOOK
COOK
COOS
COWS
SOWS
SEWS
SEES

Can you find any alternative solutions?

BRAIN GAME 89

BRAIN GAME 90

3	9	5	2	8	6	7	4	1
1	2	6	4	5	7	3	9	8
7	4	8	1	3	9	6	5	2
2	6	4	8	7	3	9	1	5
9	3	1	5	4	2	8	7	6
5	8	7	6	9	1	2	3	4
4	7	2	3	1	8	5	6	9
6	5	3	9	2	4	1	8	7
8	1	9	7	6	5	4	2	3

ALSO AVAILABLE:

ISBN 9781780556192

ISBN 9781780556185

ISBN 9781780556208

ISBN 9781780555638

ISBN 9781780554730

ISBN 9781780555621

ISBN 9781780554723

ISBN 9781780555409

ISBN 9781780553146

ISBN 9781780553078

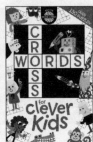

ISBN 9781780553085

ISBN 9781780552491